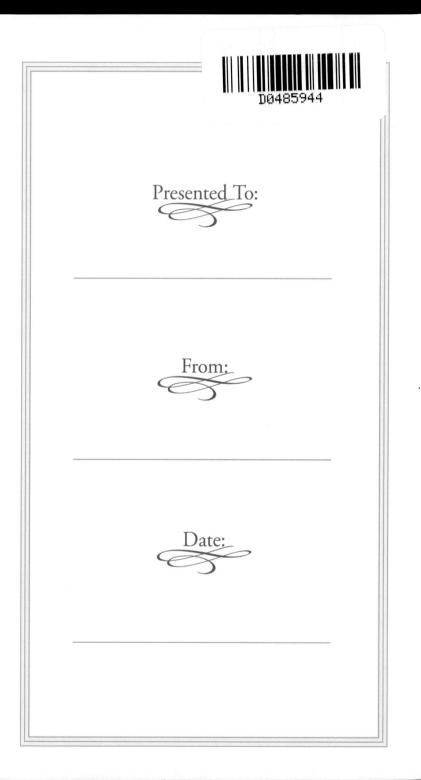

Presented To:

_____

From:

_____

Date:

_____

The Lovesick God

The Lovesick God

Answering the Deepest Longings of Your Soul

PABLO PÉREZ

DESTINY IMAGE® PUBLISHERS, INC.

P.O. Box 310, Shippensburg, PA 17257-0310

"Promoting Inspired Lives."

This book and all other Destiny Image, Revival Press, MercyPlace, Fresh Bread, Destiny Image Fiction, and Treasure House books are available at Christian bookstores and distributors worldwide.

For a U.S. bookstore nearest you, call **1-800-722-6774.**

For more information on foreign distributors, call **717-532-3040.**

Reach us on the Internet: **www.destinyimage.com.**

ISBN 13 TP: 978-0-7684-3979-3

ISBN 13 Ebook: 978-0-7684-8931-6

For Worldwide Distribution, Printed in the U.S.A.

1 2 3 4 5 6 7 8 9 10 11 / 13 12 11

Dedication

Once upon a time, there was a beautiful little girl who met a charming but inexperienced boy. Her radiance so captured the boy's affections that at night he would whisper to the Father of Lights, requesting permission to have her forever.

That famous city of the south, Buenos Aires, still remembers the day they fell in love—it happened at the end of a century, when prophecies converged and dreams of eternity gripped the earth. The inexperienced boy *asked*—the beautiful little girl said *yes*—and the adventurous journey of lovers begun.

As years went by, love was tested. The storms of life clashed against them (one after the other) and the boy developed a severe infirmity of the soul. In fact, when his pain levels escalated he tried to abandon the Father of Lights, and forsake ever knowing Him. But the little girl rescued him from his foolishness. She never gave up, never stopped loving him; even though the boy often wounded her, she pursued him with love and saved him from self-destruction countless times.

Their love story continues; some believe it will never end. One thing is for sure, she's truly something. *I should know.*

To that beautiful little girl, *Andrea*, the grown-up boy dedicates this book—I want the world to know *how much I love you, how grateful I am for all your kindness, and that I am forever yours.*

Endorsements

If you want to experience the deep emotions of God's heart and discover secrets that can awaken your soul, read this book. As is Pablo's music, so is his writing—majestic, powerful, and life-changing.

Mike Bickle
International House of Prayer

Unpretentious, nonreligious, powerful, and life-changing—a must-read. The only disappointment about this book is it is too short! No doubt Pablo Pérez has so much more to bring by His Spirit.

Rory Alec
Cofounder, God TV

This book grapples with some of the soul's most fundamental longings. "Who am I?" "Why am I alive?" "What is my ultimate inner cry?" Discover how the great reach of the human heart is satisfied in a breathtaking romance with the King of all hearts. Reading this book will take you on a daring adventure with the Bridegroom God.

Bob Sorge
Secrets of the Secret Place

Contents

CHAPTER ONE

Forever Thirsty

"I'm leaving for Kenya, Africa…in two hours."

My wife could not believe my words, and honestly, that Tuesday morning I wasn't thinking of traveling at all. Egypt and Mexico felt enough for a month—so I thought. But rounding 11 o'clock, while reading a book, drinking my second cappuccino, and vividly imagining the relaxing days ahead, a thunderous e-mail arrived and broke the morning in two:

Can you be in Kenya tomorrow?

The message came from Jono Hall, director of the Forerunner Media Institute at the International House of Prayer of Kansas City, where I live. Graeme

Spencer—head of production for God TV—joined the conversation from Washington, DC and asked me if I could lead worship in Kenya *that* Thursday. After 30 seconds of extreme thinking, I finished drinking my coffee and typed a hesitant *yes*.

Hours later, I pulled the airplane ticket from my smart phone and boarded flights toward Chicago and Heathrow (London) where I joined the exhausted but friendly God TV team. We ate a snack and embarked British Airlines flight 65 for Nairobi, Kenya. It was Wednesday night when I finally reached Africa.

With only three hours of sleep, I jumped into a small rented bus en route for "mountain base." This unique ride delivered 45 minutes of safari driving with some good old British chat. (Try that when you have jet lag!)

High on the mountains the morning felt intoxicating—the raw fragrance of the wild, the sun-drenched colors all around—it looked like nature dancing. Backstage, a cornfield evolved into majestic hills that culminated with crystalline skies. It was breathtaking—creation at its best, with a heavenly touch—the Watoto children's choir of Uganda rocking the whole platform.

For almost six lengthy hours, we worshiped and broadcast unrehearsed live television to the nations. Unquestionably draining, but absolutely *unforgettable!*

At sunset, we left mountain base and drove back to the hotel (through wild, bumpy roads you have not seen in the best movies). Hours later, I kissed Africa good-bye, switched a couple of airplanes in Europe, and made it back to Kansas City on Friday (for dinner).

Now, that's what I call ministry on steroids—a thrilling Kingdom adventure, the adrenaline rush of crossing continents in twenty-four hours, the awareness of God's presence upon your heart, and the superb kick of an extraordinary experience.

Uncovering the Mystery of an Irresistible Word

The paragraph above contains a compelling and captivating *word*. To be perfectly honest, I shared my trip to Kenya to highlight the significance of that *word*. I promise, understanding the *word* will help you decipher the cravings of your soul and uncover the reason for most of your victories and failures.

Imagine yourself in a place where beauty, unforgettable journeys, and thrilling adventures happen every day. Picture a life where boredom is vanished and fascination is the ruling emotion of your heart. What if you could enjoy a never-ending story within a world where romance and majesty constantly take your breath away?

Here is something few people understand: deep within our hearts we live and yearn for *experience*. All of us crave it; it's not really "things," "status," and "success" we desire, it's the *experience* those things provide that we are after—the way they make us *feel* inside.

If you wear human flesh and possess a soul (and it would be creepy if you don't), then you desire to be known and loved. You dream of beauty, romance, and fulfillment. You yearn for adventure, thrills, and fascination. You long for lasting friendships, approval, financial security, and success.

Why? Why do you want those things?

Because they *feel* great—every longing of the soul anticipates a specific experience. In fact, *experience* is the concealed driving force behind every human pursuit.

Unfortunately, the same longings are the root of our addictions. What's more, the entertainment and advertisement industries understand our cravings (and profit from them). They prey on our "emotional" shopping behaviors and cash in on our hunger for fascinating stories. *Have doubts?* Think about your favorite form of entertainment and ask: Why is it so attractive and appealing?

What's the emotional reward of the exchange? And why at times do I find myself overdoing it?

The reason we get drunk with entertainment is rather simple: *We have a profound need for mental engagement.* We need to engage and be engaged, we hunger for new discoveries and fresh encounters; it is how we are wired. The problem is that every form of entertainment ever invented becomes old. No matter how exciting, ingenious, amusing, and thrilling, we are always left wanting, always longing for more.

Something similar happens with sin, which feasts on our misguided longings. Have you ever wondered why the prohibited seems so attractive and appealing? What lies do we choose to believe when we abandon reason and agree to sin?

Truth is, you and I have crossed boundaries and tasted the forbidden. We have followed deception and irrationally searched to quench our thirst. Every time, however, after the pleasure vanishes our emptiness grows, leaving a painful trail of consequences and that revived "aroma of death."

I have lived long enough to know that *everything* within the created order comes short. Be it virtuous or evil, nothing created can cure my thirst. My craving for experience never goes away. Even thrilling ministry trips become old—they fade away, they lose their charm. On every count, I keep silently longing for more. I find my soul *forever thirsty.*

Whoever Drinks This Water Will Thirst Again

The woman said to Him, "Sir, You have nothing to draw with, and the well is deep. Where then do You get that living water? Are You greater than our father Jacob, who gave us the well, and drank from it himself, as well as his sons and his livestock?" Jesus answered and said to her, "Whoever drinks of this water will thirst again..." (John 4:11-13).

If we would run a contest for the most passionate and thirsty individual of the Old Testament, Jacob would make the top three. I mean, who else cheats his brother and father for destiny, works 14 years for the woman he loves, wins a wrestling match with the Angel of the Lord, and procreates the nation that delivers the Messiah? Only one man can brag about that.

The Samaritan woman praises the greatness of father Jacob, "the giver of the well." But Jacob's well—according to Jesus—fails to solve the human thirst dilemma. It offers a temporal solution, maybe a soft painkiller, but cannot fix our core problem.

Jacob's well is a picture of "the waters of this world." It represents every natural pleasure and painkiller for the soul ever invented. Be it the best of technology, entertainment, immorality, witchcraft, humanism, and religion—whatsoever government, culture, and devils may invent to capture the souls of men. In short, the waters of this world *cannot* and *will not* quench the profound thirst of the human heart.

Quoting Jesus, *"Whoever drinks of this water will thirst again."* I should know; I have a history with polluted wells and counterfeit water. Most of my "wells" were not sinful; actually, they had religious labels like "Success in Ministry" and "Make Your Life Count." Oh yes, some wells came in different flavors, offering innovative soul solutions. But every single one—be it religious, man-created, or from the pit of hell—soon turned shallow, disappointing, polluted, and broken. I watched my heart faint from thirst for years; the words of King Solomon became the blues of my soul: *"Everything is meaningless…completely meaningless!"* (Eccles. 1:2 NLT).

What about you? What is the well you're currently drinking from? What makes you feel great, happy, and successful? Which fountain is presently fueling your significance, establishing your "value," and defining your identity?

Perhaps the water feels too cold. Maybe you weren't ready for a direct, challenging question. *I genuinely apologize.* But believe me, more is coming. Some lines will be bone-crushing, others quite amusing, and others can potentially change your life.

I dare you to keep reading to discover the endless possibilities. Who knows what might happen within your soul?

Next: The Bold and Incredible Promise of Jesus

Let's go on a trip overseas. That's right, you and me hitting the pulse-pounding road. I told you, I make fast decisions to travel. Destination: *ancient Jerusalem.* Total expedition cost: *your creative imagination.* Coming?

Once you get to Jerusalem, drive 30 miles northwest toward Sychar (the city close to Jacob's well). Find a good tree near the well and open those ears—you're about to hear a confidential conversation between the God-Man and a forgotten woman. Within their dialogue you'll find *the secret to life* and the most meaningful words ever exchanged by two absolute strangers.

CHAPTER TWO

The Bold and Incredible Promise of Jesus

As He spoke He no longer looked to them like a lion; but the things that began to happen after that were so great and beautiful that I cannot write them. …It was only the beginning of the real story. All their life in this world and all their adventures in Narnia had only been the cover and the title page: now at last they were beginning Chapter One of the Great Story which no one on earth has read: which goes on forever: in which every chapter is better than the one before.

—C.S. Lewis, The Last Battle[1]

Eternity is written on our hearts. That's why we love stories like the one above—they remind us that life is *more* than the things we see and that we are *more* than our minds have dared to believe. Truly, we were made for God, designed to love Him and be loved by Him. The magnificence of God's person is our birthright and inheritance; we exist to be fascinated by His beauty, allured by His love—His presence is the environment we were created for.

Yet, most of us live *disconnected* from this heavenly atmosphere. We navigate through life believing lies that we were told are true, feeling rollercoaster emotions that reflect those lies, and overheating our minds with the nervous cares of this world.

As if this weren't enough, an ocean of distractions threatens our sanity. Multitudes of voices call for our attention: "Come here and find life!" "Follow me!" "Buy this; it will cure your pain." Both the media and savvy marketers have identified our thirst. They understand our emotional brain and how to intelligently seduce our longings for profit. In fact, they spend endless hours and loads of money in order to capture our attention and sell their "unique happy water."

Ironically, they are not alone in their pursuit. Although for much different reasons, the God of Heaven and the prince of darkness are after the same thing—*your burning heart.*

Make no mistake, your affections will burn for something or someone; your heart is not neutral. You must experience life at any cost, and you will. Because you carry powerful passions within, they are like mighty rivers of longing that will not relent in their search for an outlet.

Sorry if I'm breaking the news to you, but we're dealing with unfathomable soul affections and the *charm* of many lovers. This tension feels like subtle harassment; if we're not careful, we become a flute that anyone can play.

Few people understand that every input needs an output. This is why—like the Samaritan woman—we tend to quench our thirst with false lovers, switching from one fountain to the next. But it never works, and as a famous rock star would sing, "We still haven't found what we're looking for."[2]

So here we are, back with this nameless woman. Little did she know, when that unusual Middle Eastern noon arrived she would see color for the first time and her forgotten heart would be set free—forever satisfied.

How Could I Have Missed This for So Long?

> *Jesus answered and said to her, "Whoever drinks of this water will thirst again, but whoever drinks of the water that I shall give him will never thirst. But the water that I shall give him will become in him a fountain of water springing up into everlasting life"* (John 4:13-14).

Having identified "the waters of this world" and some of our deep longings, let's now focus on the bold promise of Jesus: *If you drink My water you will never thirst again.*

I don't know about you, but my first reaction would be: "Wait, Lord, I need clarification. Do You mean never thirsting again now, or when I get to Heaven? You see, last time I checked I was still profoundly thirsty. The day I got saved—well, I think every pastor's kid is a little confused about that—but You know I witnessed four revivals in three nations and have served in ministry for almost two decades. I have been around the block, so to speak, and it feels great when You are close, but honestly…the 'never thirsting again' part has escaped me."

Perhaps Jesus would answer: "Pablo, I appreciate your honesty, but you're missing the forest for the trees. First, you need to identify *who* the water is. Next, you must understand what *drinking* the water means. Then, you must comprehend the unlimited extent of the phrase *'will become in him a fountain of water springing up into eternal life.'* Have you discerned the meaning of eternal life? And how, by constantly drinking, the water becomes a fountain within you that never runs dry? By the way, was the Samaritan woman in Heaven when I told her that? Look, it's very simple. Like most of My people, you already have 'the water' within, but only drink from it occasionally. And though you have witnessed My glory and the power of My presence, you often switch back to your 'broken cisterns,' those 'God replacements' you treasure. Then, after drinking what makes you miserable, your thirst is revived and you think that My promise does not work. Look, I really like you. But you should listen again to what I said and follow My instructions."

Intriguing. As Spock would observe, *fascinating.* How could I have missed this for so long? When I consider all the years wasted and every single excuse embraced, I can't help but *kick* myself. What's more, the day I understood what I'm about to tell you, my burnout excuses died. They were terminated; not a single wire within my brain can accept them anymore.

Jesus was not playing with her and He's not playing with us. His promise remains. *If we drink the water He gives we will never thirst again*—this applies to *today* and to all eternity. It is a bold and incredible promise which raises two logical questions: *"Who or what is the water?"* and *"What does it mean to drink it?"*

Give Me This Water, So I Won't Thirst Again

> *The woman said to Him, "Sir, give me this water, that I may not thirst, nor come here to draw." Jesus said to her, "Go, call your husband, and come here." The woman answered and said, "I have no husband." Jesus said to her, "You have well said, 'I have no husband,' for you have had five husbands, and the one whom you now have is not your husband; in that you spoke truly"* (John 4:15-18).

Not that she understood the magnitude of the offer, but something in His voice probably awakened her heart, so she asked, "Give me this water so I won't thirst again."

Jesus shot straight to the heart and said something like, "Sure; I'm glad you asked. But before I give you My water we must deal with the 'water' you are currently drinking. Go call your husband and come back."

She froze inside; chances are she forgot to breathe while responding, *"I have no husband."* The story continues with an impressive hook-undercut (mail-reading) by Jesus. Thing is, she turned out to be living with "number six."

If there is something we can't accuse her of, it's being hopeless. After five broken marriages and loads of emotional wounds, she did not give up. Yes, her sixth attempt was definitely adultery, but we should give her credit for maintaining high hopes and still trying, don't you think?

Contrary to some popular scholarly trends, I believe her core problem is not immorality. That was just a sinful output, merely the *symptom* of a far greater disease. The central issue, which Jesus brilliantly addressed, is the same every living human being has—*we desperately thirst within.* The Samaritan woman jumped from one relationship to another trying to find what only God can give.

We are not unlike her when we place impossible expectations on friendships and family and (unconsciously) demand they solve our emptiness; or when we search for the perfect community (the ideal local church or that truly *loving* ministry team) because the last seven we visited didn't work, and someone told us (though we can't really remember who) that all believers should always behave flawlessly and be faultless.

Let's go back to Sychar now.

Jesus brought up the whole "husband" issue not to condemn but to *enlighten*. She had to recognize the false lovers that were capturing her soul, and she did. She refused to present excuses and agreed with Jesus, qualifying herself to receive the *real* water—the water Jesus gives.

Living Human Beings and Two Types of Thirst

Before going further, I would like to explain two concepts. First, what I mean by a term I used earlier: *living human being*. Second, I want to explain the difference between two kinds of thirst.

Living human beings—Sadly, some folks have totally killed their capacity to thirst. Yes, they still breathe, but they are not alive. Some are victims of abuse and tragedy; others have drowned within the ocean of bitterness and despair; still many others are buried under the burdensome slavery of religious systems. I pray God may use this book to revive them, so they would *live* again and fully experience the fire of His love.

Two types of thirst—When teaching the Beatitudes Jesus said, *"Blessed are those who hunger and thirst for righteousness, for they shall be filled"* (Matt. 5:6). Thirsting for righteousness is *not* the thirst I've been talking about, and it's obviously *not* the thirst Jesus cures forever. For example, I can sing *"As the deer pants for streams of water, so my soul pants for you, O God"* (Ps. 42:1 NIV) and be totally satisfied from my Samaritan type of thirst, because what I'm basically saying is: *I want more of You, God. I'm lovesick. I cannot live without Your embrace. Let me know You more; let me feel Your love.* Consequently, I can thirst for righteousness and also never thirst again. The concept will be clearer as we move on.

Next: Perhaps the Greatest Secret of the Universe

On the coming pages we'll discover the identity of "the water" Jesus gives and what "drinking" the water means.

But things will only get better afterward, because the purpose of drinking is the unfolding of *eternal life*, and it's not what most people think it is.

Endnotes

1. C.S. Lewis, *The Last Battle* (New York, NY: HarperCollins, 1984), 210-211.

2. Paraphrase of U2's, "I Still Haven't Found What I'm Looking For," from album entitled, *The Joshua Tree*, 1987, released by Island Records (music by U2, lyrics by Bono).

CHAPTER THREE

Perhaps the Greatest Secret of the Universe

*O living flame of love that tenderly wounds my soul
in its deepest center!...How gently and lovingly you
wake in my heart, where in secret you dwell alone;
and in your sweet breathing, filled with good and
glory, how tenderly you swell my heart with love.*

—John of the Cross[1]

Back in those days, during winter of 1991 to be exact, Buenos Aires felt intoxicatingly beautiful. Everything seemed radiant and glowing. It was still the same city—packed with tall buildings, tons of busy people and nerve-wracking noises—but the eyes of my heart had evolved somehow. *I was not the same.*

It happened during weeks of ruthless fever, after I became totally immobilized and sentenced to my Bible-college bed. When my defenses were "literally" down and I wondered the meaning of it all, a voice emerged from within and said: *If you give Him room I will completely revolutionize your life*.

Things got moving when Andrea, who by then had already stolen my heart, gave me a skinny book titled, *Good Morning, Holy Spirit*, written by Benny Hinn.[2] I didn't know Benny back then and definitely wasn't a fan of that hairstyle from the '70s, but his message made my soul *burn*. It was the first time I heard about the person of the Holy Spirit in such a direct way.

Soon after, I began speaking to the Holy Spirit as a Person, and amazingly He started talking back. The sound of His voice, His companionship, and the flame of His love were like nothing I'd experienced before. I was transformed. *My life literally changed in a matter of weeks*.

But not all was well in Camelot. As the years went on, I grew cold and forsook Him, still doing ministry and going through the motions but without His flame burning inside. At times my *thirst* would become unbearable—I would awake from my slumber and return to Him, only to forget Him again during the heat of life's battles, when seasons change unannounced and doors painfully close.

Maybe you already guessed it, or perhaps you knew from the beginning. If you didn't, I'm quite sure you have figured it out by now. He is *the water* that cures our thirst, the *key* that solves the human dilemma—the Holy Spirit *is* the living water Jesus gives.

> …*"If anyone thirsts, let him come to Me and drink. He who believes in Me, as the Scripture has said, out of his heart will flow rivers of living water." But this He spoke concerning the Spirit, whom those believing in Him would receive; for the Holy Spirit was not yet given, because Jesus was not yet glorified* (John 7:37-39).

The day you truly believed, that day when you first came to Jesus, God regenerated your soul and gave you His Spirit. I am not talking about the baptism of the Holy Spirit (that powerful Pentecost experience of Acts 2). It could be that you got the baptism of the Spirit the day you were saved, but maybe not. What I'm highlighting, however, is the *indwelling of the Holy Spirit within your heart.* That "indwelling" became a reality the instant God reached you with salvation.

Not that the disciples were saved here, but this event after the resurrection (and way before Pentecost) illustrates my point:

> *So Jesus said to them again, "Peace to you! As the Father has sent Me, I also send you." And when He had said this, He breathed on them, and said to them, "Receive the Holy Spirit"* (John 20:21-22).

If we have been born again and already posses the "water" that cures our thirst, *how come we are still thirsty?* How come millions of Christians worldwide are bored to death, flirting with sin, drinking from broken cisterns, and feeling absolutely unhappy?

The answer is simple—we are not drinking the Water.

Once more, here is the bold promise of Jesus: *"whoever drinks of the water that I shall give him will never thirst…"* (John 4:14).

The promise is in the drinking, not in the ownership. The ownership makes you a son of God, but the *drinking* cures your thirst and meets the deep longings of your soul. Put differently, possessing the water is not enough; you must drink the water to inherit the promise—and not just drink it one time, or during a special conference, or while the heavens are opened and a national revival sweeps the land. All that is fantastic, but to take hold of Jesus' promise, we must drink the water every single day. It's *the tree of life* in the midst of Eden kind of deal—you must keep eating (see Gen. 3:22-23).

Therefore, if the water Jesus gives is the Holy Spirit, what does it mean to drink that water? *I'm glad you asked.*

Drinking the Water Jesus Gives

> *The amazing grace of the Master, Jesus Christ, the extravagant love of God, the intimate friendship of the Holy Spirit, be with all of you* (2 Corinthians 13:14 MSG).

I love the way Paul finishes his second letter to the Corinthians, mentioning three foundational pillars of the Christian life: the grace of the Lord Jesus Christ, the love of God, and the fellowship of the Holy Spirit.

There's so much to write about those three. Actually, we'll dive deep into the second pillar down the road. But let me tell you, the mystery of the first two is solved by practicing the third—the one I enjoy calling *the greatest secret of the universe.*

There's so much chat about the universe today. Different fields of science are going ballistic with new data and discoveries. One of my hobbies is to learn the basics of quantum physics, neuroscience, advanced theoretical physics, nonlinear dynamics, subatomic energy, and the study of frequency. It's fascinating to watch how scientists discover what God has hidden and draw the same conclusion: *There is an infinite intelligent mind behind every single detail in the universe.*

I'm not a scientist of course, but in my modest *quantum* opinion, new discoveries and historic "aha" moments will never surpass what I consider to be the greatest secret of the universe—*living in fellowship with the Holy Spirit.*

After all, on creation day the Spirit of God was hovering over the face of the waters, and He's responsible for raising Jesus from death (not a small task). Shocking as it sounds, the Holy Spirit lives somewhere between my belly and my brain, and I can converse with Him 24/7 and enjoy His companionship. Plus, I can walk in His incredible power, acquire His ageless wisdom, and dive into the ocean of His affections.

It's worth repeating: The bold and incredible promise of Jesus is in the *drinking*. And this is what "drinking the water" means—living in intimate friendship and fellowship *with* the Person of the Holy Spirit.

> *The Comforter (Counselor, Helper, Intercessor, Advocate, Strengthener, Standby), the Holy Spirit, Whom the Father will send in My name [in My place, to represent Me and act on My behalf], He will teach you all things. And He will cause you to recall (will remind you of, bring to your remembrance) everything I have told you* (John 14:26 AMP).

Fellowship with the Spirit of Truth, as Jesus calls Him, is the secret to never thirsting again. The Holy Spirit counsels, strengthens, and teaches us all things. By following His "law of life," we are constantly delivered from the law of sin and death.

Not only that, but the power of His presence brings conviction to the world and works miracles to endorse the message of the Gospel. In addition, the fire of His love answers our deep longings and heals the wounds of our soul.

But all of that is only the beginning.

The Holy Spirit reveals the deep things of God and unveils the majesty of Jesus and the glory of the Father.

> *But, as it is written, "What no eye has seen, nor ear heard, nor the heart of man imagined, what God has prepared for those who love him"—these things God has revealed to us through the Spirit. For the Spirit searches everything, even the depths of God* (1 Corinthians 2:9-10 ESV).

The bold and incredible promise of Jesus doesn't end with us; it ends with Him in full union with us. That's what our souls were designed for, that's what we truly crave—*full union with God*. As we continue to drink, His water becomes a fountain which springs up unto eternal life where we encounter the unfolding of God's emotions, the power of His love, and the fascinating beauty of the Lovesick God.

Living in fellowship with the Holy Spirit is the key to life. He not only unlocks our hearts, cures our thirst, and heals our souls, but He opens the treasure of the deep things of God. For all of this and a million more reasons, I consider His fellowship the greatest secret of the universe.

Eternal Life Is
Not Entirely What You Think

Who drinks the water I shall give him, says the Lord, will have a spring inside him welling up for eternal life. Let them bring me to your holy mountain in the place where you dwell. Across the desert and through the mountain to the Canyon of the Crescent Moon, to the Temple where the cup that holds the blood of Jesus Christ resides forever.[3]

Since long before anybody can remember, the human race has been dreaming of immortality and eternal life. The quote above is not from the Bible, of course, it's from the movie *Indiana Jones and the Last Crusade*.

The dream of "living forever" has filled countless fiction novels, plays, and movie theaters. Throughout history, immortality has filled the thoughts of emperors and world leaders, as proven by their "treasure hunting efforts" to locate the *fountain of youth* and other famous religious artifacts.

Very amusing when you think about it, since every one of us will exist forever, the only question is *where*.

Yes, the real estate experts have it right—*location, location, location*.

According to the Bible, we are immortal beings. Our human spirit will never be destroyed, no matter if we choose Jesus or reject Him. Receiving God's grace determines our relationship with Him and our everlasting *location*, not our eternal existence. All of humanity *is* and will ever *be*. Once more, the important question is *where* it will *be*.

Next:
The Everlasting Encounter

Eternal life is not just living forever. The famous memorized verse reveals: *"God so loved the world that He gave His only begotten Son, that whoever believes in Him should not perish but have everlasting life"* (John 3:16). Perishing is not spiritual annihilation and "eternal life" is not simply your unfair ticket to Heaven.

It's way more—immeasurably, exceedingly more.

Endnotes

1. "The Living Flame of Love," from John of the Cross Selected Writings (Mahwah, NJ: Paulist Press,

1987), 293-294, http://books.google.com/books?id
=2D3dOcBlbs8C&pg=PA285&dq=the+living+fl
ame+of+love&hl=en&ei=CMjqTcvHNpS8sQPI5
_D_DQ&sa=X&oi=book_result&ct=result&resnum=
10&ved=0CF4Q6AEwCQ#v=onepage&q=living%20
flame%20of%20love&f=false (accessed June 4, 2011).

2. Benny Hinn, *Good Morning, Holy Spirit* (Nashville,
   TN: Thomas Nelson, 2004).

3. *Indiana Jones and the Last Crusade*, dir. Steven
   Spielberg, perf. Harrison Ford (Paramount Pictures,
   1989), DVD.

CHAPTER FOUR

The Everlasting Encounter

We are half-hearted creatures, fooling about with drink and sex and ambition when infinite joy is offered us, like an ignorant child who wants to go on making mud pies in a slum because he cannot imagine what is meant by the offer of a holiday at the sea.

—C.S. Lewis, The Weight of Glory[1]

That Middle Eastern sun was not helping. Smitten by sweat and blushing she wondered, *How can He know so much?* It seemed right to change gears—a scandalous adultery and five old broken marriages were not a lot of fun to talk about. Gathering her courage she said, *"Sir, I perceive that You are a prophet"* (John 4:19), thereby engineering the most unique conversation twist of the Gospels.

However haphazardly and seemingly out of the blue, the Samaritan woman switched the discussion to the topic of "worship." Perhaps it was automatic, since the correct religious assumption would be to connect worship with prophets. But there is another possibility—what if she was *drinking* living water for the first time? What if something within her started bubbling up? If that's the case, *worship* became a necessity, a pathway toward divine discovery.

> *Woman, believe Me, the hour is coming when you will neither on this mountain, nor in Jerusalem, worship the Father....The hour is coming, and now is, when the true worshipers will worship the Father in spirit and truth; for the Father is seeking such to worship Him* (John 4:21,23).

Two mountains were controlling worship liturgy in that region—Mount Zion (Jerusalem) and Mount Gerizim (Samaria). Jesus set the record straight by pointing to Jerusalem as the right place of worship and explaining how salvation comes from the Jews. Then He prophesied about a coming hour when a new breed of worshipers—*true worshipers*—would worship the Father in spirit and truth, and that His Father was seeking such to worship Him.

The quality of the information released is mind-blowing. Equally incredible, however, is why Jesus chose to deliver such historic revelation to a *Samaritan*. Samaritans were considered impure, dirty, and close to animals in Jewish eyes.

To make it worse, she was a woman. The simple act of Jesus talking to her caught the disciples by surprise. But even more tormenting to the dull religious mind is the fact she was still living in adultery when Jesus told her this! None of the other Gospels captured Jesus going to Samaria, much less the conversation. And, in all likelihood, John learned the dialogue details from her, later on.

What's the big deal? Well, *God is the big deal!* He trusts a significant *New Covenant* revelation to an ex-adulterous, brand-new believer. If you were God, would you operate like this? Would I? Obviously, God is *not* into the snobbish trend of most educational religious systems. He's definitely challenging admission and promotion rules. No wonder Jesus storms upon the confident Pharisees, "…*Assuredly, I say to you that tax collectors and harlots enter the kingdom of God before you*" (Matt. 21:31).

The Key to the Knowledge of God

I can only imagine what went through her mind; one thing is sure, there are no coincidences in Scripture. Pay attention to the sequence—thirst, counterfeit water, living water, drinking that living water, a fountain springing up, worship, and:

> *The woman said to Him, "I know that Messiah is coming" (who is called Christ). "When He comes, He will tell us all things." Jesus said to her, "I who speak to you am He"* (John 4:25-26).

Like following a heavenly symphony, the word *Messiah* comes out of her mouth. How outstanding! Pause and imagine the effect of the *Messiah* word in the atmosphere. Chances are Jacob's well had earthquake thoughts and the angels guessed, *"Is He going to tell her? Will He reveal Himself? Can He resist this enthralling fragrance of worship?"*

Jesus would often leave people wondering, but not this time. The whole exchange needed a grand finale. It was like a perfect canvas looking for completion. He peered into her gleaming eyes and declared: *I who speak to you am He.*

She was speechless. It took more than her breath away. Leaving her water jar, she ran back to town and boldly spread the news about Jesus, positioning herself as the first "Gentile" evangelist.

The sequence of the story is powerful, and rather fascinating in how *worship* happens minutes before the revelation of Jesus. It's not a coincidence of course, because fellowship with the Holy Spirit grows within a lifestyle of worship. Worship *is* the key to the knowledge of God—the pathway that prepares us to experience the Lovesick God.

A brief quiz: If you want a personal appointment with the King of the universe, and you happen to know what He's searching for, what would be the logical thing to do?

Why the Father Seeks for Worshipers

When we truly engage our hearts and focus on the Lord, we will encounter Him—this is precisely what He wants. It is why the Scripture often says, *"Sing to the Lord, all the earth…"* and *"From the rising of the sun to its going down the Lord's name is to be praised"* (1 Chron. 16:23; Ps. 113:3). It is also the reason why the Father is searching for true worshipers. You see, He wants to be *encountered*.

Why does God desire to be encountered? The answer is a bit extensive, but here are some revealing clues.

From the very beginning, God is after relationship; He longs to be known, loved, and preferred. He could have programmed you to choose Him, but love without choice is not love at all. So He gave you free will, taking the risk of suffering your rejection and independence. Nonetheless, He never stops pursuing you; even though He is often misunderstood and has to compete with other lovers, He anticipates and longs for the day you will choose Him voluntarily—not only to escape the wages of sin, but because He has stolen your heart.

In simple words: God longs to be encountered, to reveal Himself, and to awaken the living flame of love within your soul. (True lovers can testify—hearts are ravished by true encounters.)

Eternal Life—The Unfolding of God's Personality

And this is eternal life: [it means] to know (to perceive, recognize, become acquainted with, and understand) You, the only true and real God, and [likewise] to know Him, Jesus [as the] Christ (the

*Anointed One, the Messiah), Whom You have
sent* (John 17:3 AMP).

You'll be surprised to learn that when you constantly drink the water Jesus gives (fellowship with the Holy Spirit) the possibilities for divine encounter become endless. The engulfing presence of the Spirit becomes a fountain that springs up into eternal life. *And what is eternal life?*

Jesus tells us clearly in John, *"And this is eternal life, that they may know You, the only true God, and Jesus Christ whom You have sent"* (John 17:3). Eternal life is getting to know the Father and the Son. It is the knowledge of God's personality, the unveiling of God's beauty, and the understanding of *why* He's beautiful.

Eternal life is the main gift Jesus came to give. It is the reason He died for our sins on the Cross, rose again from the grave, and ascended to Heaven. Eternal life is also *why* He will return to Earth—to fulfill His destiny and fill the earth with the knowledge of the glory of God, as the water covers the sea (see Isa. 11:9; Hab. 2:14).

Eternal life is the reason the Father sent the Helper (the promised Holy Spirit) who cures our thirst and declares everything about Jesus, even the deep things of God.

Eternal life is where the fountain springs up to—the ever-increasing knowledge of God exploding within you, tenderizing your heart, changing your emotional chemistry, and renewing your marvelous mind.

Eternal life is *the everlasting encounter* with the Lovesick God.

Next: A Bridegroom God in Love With a Harlot

The journey is set. From now on every page will lead you to encounter the majesty of the Lovesick God.

The most excellent song ever written is true; He is altogether lovely—and I will do my best to show you *why*.

Endnote

1. C.S. Lewis, *The Weight of Glory* (San Francisco, CA: HarperCollins, 2001), 26.

CHAPTER FIVE

A Bridegroom God in Love With a Harlot

Go again [Hosea], *love a woman who is loved by a lover and is committing adultery, just like the love of the Lord for the children of Israel, who look to other gods and love the raisin cakes of the pagans* (Hosea 3:1).

In all likelihood, the prophet pondered in amazement. Waves of intense sorrow and passion engulfed his soul. His mind remained confused, anxiously reasoning for logic.

Go again? Love her again?

The woman—Gomer, *the prostitute*. Her story—*scandalous and unprecedented*. God commanded Hosea to marry a prostitute and have children of prostitution (see Hos. 1:2). Tossing his reputation through the window, he obeyed the Lord and married Gomer—*a common harlot*—the future mother of his children.

Did Hosea fall in love with her? Sure, after a while. But his redeeming love suffered when Gomer abandoned the house, the kids, and the prophet. We are short on details of when, how, and why. Maybe it was too painful for the author (Hosea) to elaborate. But this is sure—Gomer embraced the wounds of her soul, went astray, and played the harlot with many lovers.

Why did she leave? Why did Gomer run away after tasting so much good? Good question! Our ex-harlot, runaway wife, and harlot-again draws a striking picture, one that you and I know very well. She is a portrait of the fallen heart; she illustrates the backsliding and adulterous tendencies of our souls.

After tasting the bitter wine of betrayal, the prophet learned to love as God loves and experienced the complexity of His desire for humans. The dramatic journey of

Hosea and Gomer introduces the Lord of Heaven—the supreme King of the universe—as the Lovesick God, the Bridegroom God.

> *"Therefore, behold, I will allure her, will bring her into the wilderness, and speak comfort to her. I will give her her vineyards from there, and the Valley of Achor as a door of hope; she shall sing there, as in the days of her youth, as in the day when she came up from the land of Egypt. And it shall be, in that day," says the Lord, "that you will call Me 'My Husband,' and no longer call Me 'My Master...'"* (Hosea 2:14-16).

Understanding God as a Bridegroom is crucial. You can *only* see yourself as the Bride of Christ by knowing and encountering the affections of the Bridegroom God. It's by beholding the Bridegroom that we discover our identity as His cherished Bride. Actually, the only reason there is a Bride at all is because there was first a Bridegroom—it all started with God and His burning heart.

The Creator and His Burning Heart

> *Then God said, "Let Us make man in Our image, according to Our likeness…." So God created man in His own image; in the image of God He created him; male and female He created them"* (Genesis 1:26-27).

The Lord formed you in His own image. Man and woman are wonderfully made from the dust into His own likeness. We are the marvelous display of God's infinite power and glory.

This is fabulous! But have you ever wondered *why*, why did He do it? Why did God create man?

Pause for a second and consider: God, who knows all things and dwells in eternity without time, the Beginning without beginning who (according to Isaiah 46:9-10) sees and declares the end from the very start—*didn't He know His image-bearers would fall from grace?* Of course! God foreknew Adam, Eve, the serpent, Hosea, Gomer, Israel, and the entire drama from the first family until the end of the age. The omniscient God knows it all.

Yet, in Eden He breathed His life and man became a living being. Why? Why the trouble? Why take the risk of granting free will? What was the all-sufficient and ever-knowing God looking for? Is it possible to discover His motive for creating us?

Was God bored? Did He create out of boredom or was He fueled by desire? If we decide to rule out divine boredom, then it is fair to wonder what kind of passion fueled His creative power. It is very important for us to know the answer. It matters *greatly*.

What about Calvary? Why did Jesus die on that Cross? We know enough about the benefits (what was accomplished), including the need to supply redemption for a dying race and vindicate the Father's justice. But we know very little about the *why*. The *why* of the Cross must be felt to be understood—it unveils the pinnacle of God's emotions and reveals the motives of His heart.

A suggestion: during your conversation with the Holy Spirit today, ask Him, *Why did You create me? Why did Jesus die on that Cross?* Ask, and take the time to listen. I could tell you what I believe, but it will quench the moment. My purpose here is to awaken your divine curiosity and perhaps unlock the eternity that is written on your heart.

One thing I'm sure of: it would be ironical and absolutely meaningless if you and I are the outcome of a mathematically bored God. The God I know yearns deeply; He passionately pursues and desires; *He is a Bridegroom God*—beauty, love, and romance burn deep within His heart.

The Most Important Question of Your Life

Seven hundred years after Hosea and Gomer, in the region of Caesarea Philippi, 12 ordinary men enjoyed the challenging adventure of following the God-Man. Right after 41 months of incredible miracles and powerful Kingdom teaching, they seemed ready; it was time for a test.

Jesus knew the hearts of men—the envy, the coming betrayal, the secret assassination plot. Trouble waited on the horizon. It was time to ask a very important question. The right answer to this question would establish the foundation of a world-changing movement and shape the minds of billions to come:

> …*"Who do men say that I, the Son of Man, am?" So they said, "Some say John the Baptist, some Elijah, and others Jeremiah or one of the*

prophets." He said to them, *"But who do you say that I am?"* (Matthew 16:13-15)

Peter, that big-mouth, brave fisherman, scored big time: *"You are the Christ, the Son of the living God"* (Matt. 16:16). What a moment! Peter's response opened the door for tremendous promises—on church building, the gates of hell, and Kingdom keys—but *the question* Jesus presented deserves a lot more of our attention. It's no ordinary query; it comes loaded with wisdom and revelation.

Imagine Jesus asking you, *"Who do you say that I am?"*

Here are some thought-provoking questions: Who is Jesus? What is He like? How does He feel most of the time? Is He mostly sad or mostly happy? Is He frustrated and grieved when thinking of you or is He smiling? How does Jesus feel toward you right now? Your answers (consciously or unconsciously) have been and are *shaping* your life.

Another colorful word to illustrate my point is *paradigm*. A paradigm is like a pair of lenses we use to filter the world and process data, including all present, past, and future information. Paradigms are wired mindsets. Mindsets are ideas. Ideas determine how we think, feel, and why we behave the way we do.

Our paradigm of God is the *most relevant* thing in our lives. Because the way we process Him affects our emotional life and everything we *are* and *do*.

As we approach the end of the age, a paradigm shift will take place in the minds of the redeemed. How we perceive the personality of God and how we imagine He perceives us will significantly change.

The Paradigm Shift That Marks This Generation

"I will allure her, will bring her into the wilderness, and speak comfort to her…and it shall be, in that day," says the Lord, "that you will call Me 'My Husband,' and no longer call Me 'My Master'" (Hosea 2:14,16).

God is mostly perceived as a taskmaster, somehow good but demanding and unfair at the core. Even believers often view Him as a supreme boss who only seeks to get the job done. Others see Him as highly irritable (cold, distant, and short-tempered), ready to punish every imperfection.

This perspective of God is *wrong*. It is a distorted and harmful view that keeps the souls of men in bondage. Satan knows this well; his network of demons works over time to endorse those lies in people's minds. He's the ultimate accuser—constantly accusing God's personality to our hearts.

But God has a plan. Darkness cannot remain when the light of God's countenance shines. The Holy Spirit is unveiling the knowledge of God's Person in unprecedented ways. What Hosea predicted will take place: *"In that day…you will call Me 'My Husband,' and no longer call Me 'My Master'"* (Hos. 2:16).

No longer will the Lord be seen as a cold taskmaster but as a passionate and loving Husband. (Of course, the Hebrew word for "my master" is *Baali*,[1] which deals with Israel's addiction to spiritual harlotry.) But my point here is the future generation Hosea foresaw and how they will experience a paradigm shift and call God "my Husband"—a future generation that would abandon lesser lovers, return to the Lord, and fully embrace their identity as the Bride of Christ.

We are *that generation*.

The Global Emergence of Bridal Worship

From the womb of the morning, even as the rising light of dawn, the revelation of the Bridegroom God will shine across the nations and redefine the identity of the Church. This Bridegroom "awareness" will awaken holy passion—a kind of passion that the world at large has not yet seen.

I call it *bridal worship*—a powerful expression of love and devotion that only lovesick hearts can give.

> *The Spirit and the Bride say, "Come."…And let the one who is thirsty come; let the one who desires take the water of life without price.* (Revelation 22:17 ESV).

Bridal worship is the overflow of souls that have encountered the Heavenly Bridegroom. Engulfed by fiery affections, they can't help but call God "my Husband" as Hosea predicted. Like the sound of many waters in the open fields and stadiums of the earth, millions will sing the song of the Bride and hear the song of the Bridegroom.

Bridal worship is the passionate response of a people fascinated by divine beauty, ruined by love, and changed by the burning desire of God. Bridal worship flows from a heart enflamed by bridal affections, lost in the ocean of divine desire, having found superior and eternal pleasures in Jesus.

Bridal worship will ignite the end-time revival and release the fiery zeal of God's love on a global scale. It will ease the atmosphere for unprecedented signs and wonders—the sick will be healed, the demon-possessed will be free, and the dead will be raised. Bridal worship will sweep across the planet, leaving millions of souls lovesick for Jesus Christ.

Men and the Bride of Christ Language

I get it—men tend to feel uncomfortable with this bridegroom-bride romantic language. "Leave that flaky-goofy bridegroom stuff for the women," they say.

We guys enjoy wild dangerous battles with lots of blood and thrilling adventures. But listen—*would you feel better if I remind you that Jesus is not only a Bridegroom?* He is also a returning Judge and conquering King—the ultimate end-of-the-age Warrior who fights extreme battles (with tons of blood) and triumphs to enjoy a never-ending adventure. Oh yes! *But here is the deal*—this powerful

King and Judge is a Bridegroom at the core. In fact, one of the reasons He rocks the planet and destroys His enemies (during those final years) is to avenge His Bride, who has been abused and martyred among the nations.

Furthermore, the doctrine of the Bride of Christ goes beyond gender; throughout the Scriptures the concept is used to highlight the most remarkable truth: *We are God's beloved and have intimate access to His heart.* Out of all the created order, we are the only ones invited to know the Lord intimately—to be loved by Him and have the pleasure of loving Him in return.

Feel the passion of God's heart:

> *I will betroth you to Me forever; yes, I will betroth you to Me in righteousness and justice, in loving-kindness and mercy; I will betroth you to Me in faithfulness, and you shall know the Lord* (Hosea 2:19-20).

Listen to this old friend of the Bridegroom:

> *...I have betrothed you to one husband, that I may present you as a chaste virgin to Christ* (2 Corinthians 11:2).

Men and women alike are betrothed to Him forever. The Lord of all creation is a Bridegroom God. He longs to be intimate with us; as I've mentioned before—love, romance, and passion burn deep within His heart.

To summarize, my brave-heart reader, you can breathe and relax. Being the Bride of Christ is not about gender. You don't have to visualize yourself coming down the aisle wearing a white dress; at least not for a while (see Rev. 19:8). Plus, the day you encounter the "romance of the Gospel" and the fire of God's love awakening your heart, no more explanation will be needed. Until that day, think of it this way—men are **the Bride** of Christ just as women are **the sons** of God.

Next: You May Not Be Who You Think You Are

Coming next, we'll dive deeper into the burning heart of God and explore how God's affections *transform* our emotions.

Many of our feelings are programmed by lies we have believed. We suffer the consequences of "deceptive thinking" every day. Only believing the truth can set us free—the truth of *who* God is, the truth of *who* we are, and of *how* God feels toward us.

Endnote

1. Biblesoft's New Exhaustive Strong's Numbers and Concordance with Expanded Greek-Hebrew Dictionary. CD-ROM. Biblesoft, Inc. and International Bible Translators, Inc. (© 1994, 2003, 2006) s.v. "Baali (also Baaliy)," (OT 1180).

CHAPTER SIX

You May Not Be Who You Think You Are

A certain woman of the wives of the sons of the prophets cried out to Elisha, saying, "Your servant my husband is dead…. And the creditor is coming to take my two sons to be his slaves" (2 Kings 4:1).

She was young, married to a son of the prophets and raising two beautiful sons. Life looked somehow promising, until tragedy struck. Without warning, her husband died. The hopeful days turned into a nightmare. Security faded away. Pain became torment, especially when she considered the rough journey ahead. *Widowhood*—the worst fear women had in ancient times.

Widowhood nurtures fear, despair, insecurity, reproach, shame, grief, disgrace, and the sense of being forgotten. With some obvious differences, the emotional framework of widowhood outlines the makeup of the wounded soul.

On the surface everything may look all right, but the cancer of spiritual widowhood is devouring the peace within—killing the sense of joy and causing all kinds of trouble. Unaware of divine affections, the wounded person represses the storm inside and plays the game of life—looking for fulfillment in all the wrong places, calling "home" what is *not* home, and finding refuge with inferior lovers. But time after time, the soul crashes against the cruel wall of disappointment and (eclipsed by a cycle of discouragement) sinks into deeper levels of despair.

Of course, some fake it better than others and the game of life continues. *But is this the way we're supposed to live?* Is this how God wants us to feel? I don't think so. It's time to admit the hidden journey of our souls and have a fresh encounter with our Maker. He has answers—*soul-delivering* answers.

Overcoming Guilt, Shame, and Reproach

"Do not fear, for you will not be ashamed…you will not be put to shame; for you will forget the shame of your youth, and will not remember the reproach of your widowhood anymore. For your Maker is your husband, the Lord of hosts is His name; and your Redeemer is the Holy One of Israel; He is called the God of the whole earth. For the Lord has called you…like a youthful wife when you were refused," says your God (Isaiah 54:4-6).

No matter your religious background, chances are you have believed *lies* concerning God's personality and His feelings for you. Those lies, often dressed as religion or culture, have determined your awareness and perception—how you process God, yourself, and everything else.

Furthermore, the way you feel today is the outcome of your thought life—a network of ideas that at some point, consciously or unconsciously, you embraced as true. Those beliefs have been controlling your emotions for a long time. *Put differently*, your present emotional chemistry has been programmed by the paradigms (ideas, mindsets) you have chosen to believe.

Suppose you discover some of your ideas of God are wrong. How do you renew your mind? What is the fastest way to reprogram your emotions? The Lord proclaims:

> …*You will forget the shame of your youth, and will not remember the reproach of your widowhood…* (Isaiah 54:4).

Starting today you can forget the shame of your youth and teach your brain to stop recreating (remembering) the guilt and reproach from yesterday. Here is how: *"For your Maker is your husband…"* (Isa. 54:5).

That tiny sentence carries a gold mine of *freedom*. Please read it over and over, again and again, until revelation explodes within and truth destroys deception.

I will tell you what delivers us from the tyranny of shame and grief—*the affections of the Bridegroom God and the truth of who we are in His eyes.* When you encounter the Bridegroom God, your emotional makeup starts to change, the fire of His love reshapes your soul, and negative emotions (guilt, shame, and reproach) lose their grip over you. The Creator (your Husband) sings the song of freedom and replaces your spiritual widowhood with confidence in His love.

It is transformation at its best; it feels like beautiful colors invading a dark world, or like falling in love for the first time—even as capturing the beauty of *eternal life*.

Forsaken No More!
Discovering Your Real Name

...You shall be called by a new name, which the mouth of the Lord will name…. You shall no longer be termed Forsaken… (Isaiah 62:2,4).

In a time where names have lost their magic and meaning, it is easy to overlook the significance they had in ancient times. Back in those days, a given name defined your identity and intended purpose, much as the names of today's cartoon superheroes describe their uniqueness or special powers.

Biblical names are mysteriously powerful. Believe me, they appear even more powerful when you write as I'm doing now—drinking a terrific Earl Grey tea at the Dan Panorama hotel, with most of Jerusalem out my window.

No, not in my imagination as I suggested in Chapter One; I'm literally here in the Holy Land.

This morning, on Shabbat, I had the privilege to awaken the dawn with live *outdoor* worship from atop the Mount of Olives, featuring Mount Zion and a gorgeous panoramic of Jerusalem on my back—quite an *indescribable* broadcast.

In the afternoon, walking down the streets of the beloved city, right at the corner of Jewish Quarter Road, I found a window with this headline "The Real You" and the following paragraph:

> A person's name expresses the essence of its bearer. The letters that make up your name are descriptions of your soul. Your Hebrew name is your spiritual call sign. Being called by your Hebrew name arouses your soul to be more manifest in your daily life.

What are the odds? "Seek and you shall find" comes to mind. Right when I'm writing about *names* I stumble into that sign. Some call it coincidence, others synchronicity—I call it walking in the greatest secret of the universe; thank You, Holy Spirit.

Now consider this. What if your real name is not Bob, Jennifer, Pedro, Maria, Hanz, Abdul, Don, Carlos, Pepe, John, Uwe, Fergus, or Susan? What if that old passport is just showing your outward identity, but your true identity is hidden within a mysterious *new* name you're not yet aware of?

According to Isaiah, God promised to give Jerusalem a new name, *one that the mouth of the Lord will give*. History tells that several decades after Isaiah, Jerusalem was destroyed by King Nebuchadnezzar of Babylon, the people of Judah went into captivity, and the land became desolate. With 70 years of imprisonment on the table, things looked quite awful and the nickname for Zion became *Forsaken*.

But the God of Israel, who often plays ten-dimensional chess and knows the end from the beginning, had a different opinion about His chosen people, and as usual, He sent the press release several generations earlier.

Fortunately, the *new name* is not exclusively for Zion. In fact, if somebody would ask me to condense the New Covenant in one word, this *new name* would make it into the top three because it brilliantly defines who we are and how God feels for us.

Can You Preach the Gospel With One Word?

So here it is—your new name (and your true identity): *"You shall no longer be termed Forsaken…but you shall be called Hephzibah…for the Lord delights in you…"* (Isa. 62:4).

Hephzibah is a Hebrew word. You may not like how it sounds (I think it sounds trendy). Whatever the case, the power of the name is in its meaning. *Hephzibah* means "my delight is in her."[1] In other words: *I delight in you; I enjoy you; I really like you.*

Hephzibah reveals what God thinks of you and how He sees you. It defines who you are—your spiritual status, importance, and significance. You might be thinking, "Impossible; you don't know who I am, my lifestyle, or what I have done." Fair enough; you have a point. But I don't think your case is worst than Israel's—they were sacrificing their kids to foreign gods (demons) back then.

Of course, that example is only viable if we measure our performance with theirs. But *Hephzibah* has nothing to do with our performance. It depends on the performance of one Man and one Man alone.

Truth is, you are *not* what the world says you are. You are *not* what your boss vented you are. You are *not* what your family, media, ex-spouse, doctor, school, government, or culture has insisted you are. You are *not* even what the devil accuses you of, and you're definitely *not* who you *feel* you are. You are *Hephzibah*—a nine-letter word that unveils your eternal beauty and the lovesick heart of God.

Hephzibah is the Gospel in one word—the incredible Good News of grace, salvation, and eternal life.

Hephzibah is like the down payment for the *New Man* reality, a central truth in the New Testament. The *New Man* is God's new creation in Christ Jesus—His ultimate masterpiece. It is who you truly are because of Jesus, because of the blood that was shed, and because you believed He is who He claims to be.

Let me tell you: something marvelous will happen the day you believe that *Hephzibah* is who you are. Your spirit longs for the glorious hour when you stop confessing your old "names" and embrace God's opinion of you. It is true. You are *not* forsaken; you are *not* forgotten; you are His delight.

Sounds incredible? Naturally, surrounded by clouds of accusation and years of deception, *Hephzibah* is a hard reality to grasp and live out. Even those who affirm to know its power are often betrayed by emotions that prove them otherwise. Nonetheless, if you truly take hold of your *new name*, you'll experience a freedom you never did before.

It will be like radiant rays of light overcoming darkness, or like falling in love all over again, even like beholding the beauty of the Lord and the meaning of *eternal life*.

Next: The Lovesick God

Imagine the Creator of the universe thinking about you right at this moment. What if you could read His thoughts and watch the expression on His face when your name comes up?

Truth is a Person—*Jesus*—and He made some unbelievable statements about His affections for you. What comes next can *transform* you. It sounds like the *Hephzibah* song but remixed and vocalized by the God- Man Himself.

Endnote

1. Biblesoft's New Exhaustive Strong's Numbers and Concordance with Expanded Greek-Hebrew Dictionary. CD-ROM. Biblesoft, Inc. and International Bible Translators, Inc. (© 1994, 2003, 2006) s.v. "Chephtsiy bahh," (OT 2657).

CHAPTER SEVEN

The Lovesick God

*Long before He laid down earth's foundations, He
had us in mind, had settled on us as the focus
of His love…* (Ephesians 1:4 MSG).

He did not die for angels when they fell. That glorious race of created beings did not qualify for His highest.
They were not worthy of divine incarnation, not worthy
of the ultimate sacrifice—not worthy of the shedding of
holy blood.

But *you* were. You and all the image-bearers are
mysteriously worthy of God's highest—worthy of His
everything. That's why the Word became flesh. Yes, a

mind-blowing reality, beyond anyone's comprehension, but true nonetheless.

Yet, some of us play religious clichés like, "It's all about God, not about me; I'm not really important." Are you serious? Have you read the Bible? The story is significantly about you too!

According to the Scriptures, one couple begins the script and another one ends it (with a spectacular and dramatic finale that reshapes the planet forever). Let me tell you, it's considerably about *you*. You are at the center of His plan and eternal destiny; you are the Bride—the object of His affections.

The Search for Greatness and Significance

What makes me great and significant?

I can sing, play the piano, produce worship albums, lead corporate worship, preach in front of thousands, write books, etc. But *not* one of those commendable things reveals my greatness and significance—they are gifts, talents, tools I have freely received (and developed) to lead people close to God and to serve this generation.

My achievements in any area also fail to define my importance. If they could, my worthiness would be subject to how well I perform or compete within the *systems* of men.

The *high* profile people I know and how well-connected I am does not establish my significance; it could be divine favor, perhaps some skill to build relationships, but is not *why* I am valuable and great.

Physical attributes, meaningful friendships, celebrity, obscurity, wealth, bankruptcy—all of these influence my emotions (I'm not from Mars), but again, none of them determine *why* I feel great and successful. When they do, I'm in trouble. In fact, if any of what I covered defines my significance, I'm scheduled for serious disappointment and breakdown.

Here's a dramatic illustration. My personal ministry could totally vanish from the public arena or reach billions of people in the years to come. Both outcomes—up or down, dead or alive—will *not* improve or downgrade my essential greatness, and they cannot change the primary reason *why* (today) I feel successful.

Those who truly believe what I'm about to share are difficult people to manipulate and control. They are not drawing their identity from *stuff* or from the praise and rejection of men anymore, but they have received the honor that comes from above, the life-changing truth that sets them free.

Then, what makes me great and significant? What defines my value and provides my sense of worth? Stay tuned. It's coming.

Time for Dinner: The Revolution Begins

Imagine tonight is your last dinner. How would you eat; what would you drink? Would you watch a movie while you eat? Would you be peaceful or stressful? How would you talk to your spouse, your children, your family, or friends? What would you think, feel, and say? Jesus experienced that. He knew it was His last supper. He was waiting and longing for the moment to show the full extent of His love and unveil the desire of His heart.

After washing the disciples' feet, the God-Man hinted at the identity of His betrayer and predicted Peter's triple denial. Then, the *revelation feast* began—chapters 14 to 17 of John's Gospel are a masterpiece of Scripture, delivering an ocean of treasures in the knowledge of God.

Like always, Jesus chose His words carefully. That dinner conversation would impact the lives of His followers forever. He made sure to be precise—no more parables or riddles, but plain and direct talk.

How Much Do You Think Jesus Loves You?

Before diving into the life-changing words of Jesus, consider the above subhead. It's a fair question. How much do you think Jesus loves you? Does He love you more or less than your neighbors? Is His affection determined by your performance? If yes, can His feelings for you change next month, when your performance diminishes? If not, what determines the measure and quality of His love for you?

Here is what Jesus revealed:

> *Just as the Father has loved Me, I have also loved you; abide in My love* (John 15:9 NASU).

You couldn't ask for a better deal. That high-voltage statement can rewire your emotional chemistry forever if you consider the implications. Jesus affirms to love you as the Father loves Him—in the same way, with the same intensity and passion, and the same fiery emotions the Father has for Him.

Have in mind that those privileged last supper attendants, the disciples, were far from perfect. Peter would deny he knew Jesus three times (sealing the denial with a couple of curse words), and the rest of the disciples would run away. What's more, a couple days before, two of them tried to secure first-class seating for eternity, leaving the other ten angry and preoccupied about who would be the first (see Matt. 20:20-28).

Obviously, the love Jesus felt for them transcended their upcoming failure and present immaturity—it was emanating from the Father's love for Him.

What kind of love and affection does the Father feel for Jesus?

Imagine it is one billion years before the foundation of the world. Surrounded by eternity (without any limitations of time or space), the uncreated Father enjoys unending friendship with His uncreated Son, feeling the power of His Holy Spirit (the living flame of love). Passionate affection and burning desire flow from the Father's heart to the Son—the same transcendent flame that one day would break the heavens to confess:

> *...the [visible] heaven was opened and the Holy Spirit descended upon Him in bodily form like a dove, and a voice came from heaven, saying,*

*You are My Son, My Beloved! In You I am well
pleased and find delight!* (Luke 3:21-22 AMP)

Amazing as it sounds, Jesus assures us that He feels
an identical passionate affection for us. Jesus loves us in
the same way the Father loves Him. And He's not exag-
gerating—He would never lie to us. When He says *"as the
Father has loved me,"* He means it.

I started this chapter by asking, "What makes me great
and significant? What defines my value and provides my
sense of worth?" Well, here is my answer.

Knowing and believing how God is lovesick for me
makes me great and significant. My value and identity
is determined by His burning heart—the anchor of my
soul is God's desire for me. Yes, I am super awesome, but
not because of the things I can do, the stuff I have, or the
gifts He has given me; I am super awesome because Jesus
feels for me the same intense desire and affection that the
Father feels for Him.

Truly believing this kind of love uncovered my true
identity. *It's Hephzibah all over again.* I am His delight. I
am His beloved. I am what He desires forever and ever.
This is who I am at the core—His constant affection is
my eternal fulfillment and ever-glorious destiny.

How Much Do You Think the Father Loves You?

You'll be delighted to learn that on the same famous evening, Jesus released some incredible information about His Father's affections for you. The following short statement escapes the casual reader, but it will not escape *you*; I will make sure of it.

> *I am in them and You are in Me. May they experience such perfect unity that the world will know that You sent Me and that You love them as much as you love Me* (John 17:23 NLT).

Incredible news; overwhelming implications! Imagine the Son praying, *"Father You have loved them as much as You love Me."*

I could ask, "What do You mean, Jesus? Are You saying the Father feels for us the same kind of affection He feels for You? I mean, You are the only begotten Son, the perfect One; shouldn't Your Father love You extremely more than me?"

He could answer, *"Pablo, My Father loves you with the exact passion and affection He has for Me. He feels for you the same burning desire He feels for Me. Yes, He loves you as much as He loves Me."*

I would reply, "This is massively unfair; it's too much; how can this be?"

He could reply, *"Do you remember John 3:16? 'For God so loved the world that He gave his only begotten Son'—My Father is Love and I am the expression of His love. It has always been His idea and His burning heart. You can't justify His love with human fairness. It doesn't work like that. My Father's love for you is not fair; it is a gift. Simply believe with all your heart that it is true and you'll begin to experience it."*

Many think of the Father as cold, distant, and unapproachable. Others, influenced by the wrong example of their earthly fathers, picture Him as selfish, abusive, absent, and uninvolved in personal matters. What's worse, some preachers portray Him like the intolerant deity that only *endures* our existence because Christ shed His blood and paid for our sins.

But according to Jesus, when the Father sees you He feels the same love that He has for His Son. *This is how much He loves you*. Whatever your current paradigm of the Father may be, your emotional life will change the day you start believing Jesus' words are true—the day you look to your reflection in the mirror and fully believing in your heart declare: *Father, thank You for loving me as much as You love Jesus.*

What Kind of God Has a Ravished Heart?

> *You have ravished my heart, my sister, my spouse; you have ravished my heart with one look of your eyes, with one link of your necklace. How fair is your love…! How much better than wine is your love, and the scent of your perfumes than all spices!"* (Song of Solomon 4:9-10)

The finest song ever written describes the Bridegroom God singing about how the Bride has ravished His heart. What kind of God has a ravished heart? Only the Lovesick God.

The "single look" symbolizes the gaze of your heart—the loving attention of your soul. Let's say you're having a very challenging day, struggling with different things, frustrated with yourself and several other folks. However, in the midst of the storm a thought comes; you choose to think about Him and cry out, *Jesus, I love You. Please help* me. That did it—a single look of your eyes—one movement of your heart toward Him is all it takes.

Here's my made-up version of that possible scenario. The Lord looks to the angels and says, "Did you see? That little weak and broken guy is clinging to Me in the midst of his struggles. He could sink into anger, depression, and bitterness, but no, he has chosen to look upon Me. I love it! It's so easy to worship Me up here, where My light and glory dwell. But he is worshiping and reaching out to Me from down below, surrounded by darkness. Gabriel! Michael! I have lost My heart again; where is it? I'm captured; I'm overcome with love."

You could say I'm over-dramatizing. That God could never be so soft, romantic, and vulnerable. Well, I've been wrong before, but I have plenty of assurance on this one—the entire Song of Songs proves I'm right.

Oh my love, you are as beautiful as Tirzah, lovely as Jerusalem, awesome as an army with banners! Turn your eyes away from me, for they have overcome me... (Song of Solomon 6:4-5).

Receiving the Affection of the Lovesick God

The fact that God is lovesick for you defines your identity and greatness. He has set His affections on you—the Creator of the universe likes you, now and forever more. Yes, you are worthy of God's highest—worthy of His everything—because He's madly in love with you. Do you realize how powerful this is?

But there's a catch—His love can become the anchor of your soul only if you would believe. That is, truly believe Jesus loves you like the Father loves Him, and the Father loves you as much as He loves Jesus, and that you can *move* His heart with one look of your eyes.

Next: The Power of Knowing and Believing

It's the core message of this book—the revelation of the Lovesick God and how you are the supreme object of His affections.

But as powerful as that truth is, I repeat: it will not change you unless you truly believe. And when I mention the term "believe," I'm not talking about intellectual assessment (which is merely agreeing); I'm talking about *hardwired faith*—a five-dimensional, interconnected belief system that receives and executes the power of the Gospel in every area of your life.

CHAPTER EIGHT

The Power of Knowing and Believing

And in the fourth watch of the night He came to them, walking on the sea (Matthew 14:25 NASU).

Around three in the morning, beaten by the waves and a defiant wind, they could not stop wondering, "How did He do it? Before He prayed, we had only five loaves of bread and two skeletal fish; how on earth did we end up feeding more than five thousand people and collecting twelve baskets of leftovers?"

What a historic day! Jesus bent the universal laws of physics and multiplied matter in front of their eyes—but the show wasn't over yet, not even close. They were scheduled for more intense paradigm shifts and *haunting* adventures.

After a time of solitude and prayer, Jesus left the mountain area to do some *sea-walking* (prior to boarding the boat). When the disciples saw "a man" walking on water, they instantly remembered all the ghost stories from the Galilean Marine Community—no one disagreed, it was a ghost! Showing admirable manhood, 12 grown men screamed their tender souls away, scared out of their wits and seriously terrified. Fortunately, Jesus ended their chaos, saying, "Have courage; it's Me!"

> *Peter said to Him, "Lord, if it is You, command me to come to You on the water." And He said, "Come!" And Peter got out of the boat, and walked on the water and came toward Jesus. But seeing the wind, he became frightened, and beginning to sink, he cried out, "Lord, save me!" Immediately Jesus stretched out His hand and took hold of him, and said to him, "You of little faith, why did you doubt?"* (Matthew 14:28-31 NASU)

You've got to love Peter; his big mouth often generated trouble, but on this case it opened the way for an amazing faith journey. He actually walked on water for a while, not *still* water, storm-agitated water (even though both scenarios are equally impossible).

Let me ask you a simple question: Have you done something like that? I haven't, not yet.

For as long as Peter believed the word of Jesus ("Come"), and for as long as he walked toward Him (focusing on Him), he bent gravity and conquered the raging storm. Quite amazing! Without question, Peter used *hardwired faith* on both counts—during his heroic walk and at his epic sinking.

What on Earth is hardwired faith? *Hardwired faith* is a term I use to describe the five dimensions of faith. The five dimensions are *thoughts, mental images, feelings, confession, and actions*. I will explore each one in the next chapter, but for now, let's return to Peter and consider his second act—*sinking at 3:25* A.M.

The Bible declares: *"Seeing the wind, he became frightened, and beginning to sink, he cried out, 'Lord, save me!'"* (Matt. 14:30 NASU).

First, Peter changed his focus from Jesus to the wind. Somehow the wind appeared more powerful than Jesus' word. Second, the raging hurricane became his internal reality and a new feeling emerged: *fear*. Third, his fear of sinking gave birth to an action: *real sinking*. Finally, the time came for his 911 confession, *"Lord, save me!"*—a very smart move after all.

True believing takes place when the five dimensions of faith are aligned and working together. It's not merely confessing or mental agreeing; it's all of you (thoughts, mental images, feelings, confession, and actions) going in one direction, positive or negative. Indeed, as Jesus would often say, *"It shall be done to you according to your faith"* (Matt. 9:29 NASU)—a basic Kingdom law which functions like clockwork, continually and for everything.

As you might imagine, when it comes to believing the burning desire of the Lovesick God, it is imperative to comprehend the five dimensions of believing (hard-wired faith). Because simply knowing how much God desires you will bring some relief, but truly *believing* His affections will change you forever.

Knowing and Believing Are Two Different Things

We have known and believed the love that God has for us. God is love, and he who abides in love abides in God, and God in him (1 John 4:16).

Knowing and believing God's desire for you will revolutionize your life. Both aspects are needed—to know and believe. Most people have experienced neither. Others have come to know but had wrong programming that prevented them from truly believing.

Knowing speaks of encounter, an intimate experience with God where you feel the warmth of His love in your entire being. This could happen while you are alone or during corporate worship—those glorious moments where you sense God's manifest presence and you can't help but melt in awe before the beauty of His majesty.

Believing speaks of the inner certainty and conviction that something is truth. As we have seen, it combines all your being (thoughts, mental images, feelings, confession, and actions).

John said: *"We have known and believed the love that God has for us"* (1 John 4:16). He experienced the nearness of Jesus; he knew His love. But he also believed His words on last supper night, and it made all the difference.

I've personally experienced the "knowing" dimension for many years. It felt great while God was touching me—the awareness of His presence, the warm of His love—but afterward, my wrong beliefs about God's emotions for me would take over. It was not until I truly believed His love that I encountered long-term emotional change. For this reason, I dare to say *knowing and experiencing His love* are not enough, because we will spend far more time with our own beliefs than with the tangible felt presence of God—it's just the way it is.

We need both dimensions—*knowing* and *believing*. Combining the power of both will transform our emotional chemistry, define who we are, and become the fuel for everything we do. Just like it happened with the Shulamite: *"I am my beloved's, and his desire is for me"* (Song of Sol. 7:10 NASU).

Coming to the end of her journey, the conquering Bride was absolutely convinced that she belonged to her Beloved and His desire was for her. Those words became her official confession, like the finest song of her soul. Truly believing the revelation of God's burning desire for her cured the cancer of meaninglessness and revealed her true identity.

It will be a glorious day—the day *you* truly believe the Maker of the universe is lovesick for you—the day *you* feel super-important and successful because you are absolutely certain that *you are the focus of His love, the object of His affections.*

The Message They Heard
Did Not Benefit Them

I mentioned it before, but it's worth repeating: Simply knowing how much God desires you will bring some relief, but *truly believing His affections will change you forever.* Wouldn't you like to receive the full benefits of being God's beloved? Why settle for fractional relief when you can enjoy total freedom?

Back in the wilderness days, the people of Israel heard the good news from Heaven, but they lacked a powerful ingredient:

> *For good news came to us just as to them, but the message they heard did not benefit them, because they were not united by faith with those who listened* (Hebrews 4:2 ESV).

What a sad and shocking reality! According to the writer of Hebrews, you can hear God's message and totally miss its benefits (unless you truly believe). What's more, you can read your Bible every morning, but if you don't insert true faith, most of its blessings will escape you—because the power of the Gospel is released when we truly believe.

> *For I am not ashamed of the gospel of Christ, for it is the power of God to salvation for everyone who believes…* (Romans 1:16).

If we don't believe a particular truth, then that truth cannot set us free because its delivering power is only activated by faith. Without faith applied, truth is like fuel without ignition, or like diamonds that were never found.

Hearing the message and missing its benefits is the sad reality of millions of churchgoers worldwide. But it doesn't have to be your reality. Not anymore.

Next: The Mystery of Hardwired Faith

Here is something worth repeating—Jesus said, "*It shall be done to you according to your faith*" (Matt. 9:29 NASU). This is a fundamental law of the Kingdom. The law is neutral and never stops. Whatever you constantly and truthfully believe will happen to you.

Prepare yourself to scale a new peak in your spiritual life. You will enjoy understanding why *hardwired faith* works and discovering how often you employ it. Take a deep breath and stretch your arms wide as I venture to explain the five dimensions of believing.

CHAPTER NINE

The Mystery of Hardwired Faith

All things are possible to him who believes
(Mark 9:23).

It's no secret. I'm using the term *hardwired* to illustrate the faith Jesus taught—the one He used to curse the fig tree and multiply food for thousands. This faith cannot be understood in one dimension, not even in 3D—only in 5D, because true faith is a fivefold process.

When five parts of your being are unified and aligned in *one* belief, the faith that moves mountains operates. Here are the five parts:

- *Thoughts*—the constant conversation within your mind. You are always generating opinions and formulating and answering questions about yourself, others, life, the past, the future, God, the devil, etc.

- *Mental Images*—your imagination, the faculty of forming mental pictures or concepts of what is not actually present to the senses. You are always watching your internal movies, and you are the producer and main character in them.

- *Feelings*—your emotions are the expression of what you believe at any given moment. They are the product of your thoughts and images. Your feelings reveal your resonance, your reverberation—in scientific terms, *your vibrational frequency*. (I'll explain these terms later in this chapter.)

- *Confession*—your words have creative power, but only when they are backed by your thoughts, images, and feelings. Confession without the first three dimensions is empty air and does not bring results.

- *Actions*—what you do; your works. Most of the time, your actions are the confirmation of your faith—what you truly believe.

As you might imagine, if you *confess* God is lovesick for you but *think* you are uniquely messed up, and then *picture* yourself as God's favorite but *feel* like a hopeless hypocrite and *act* like a slave who never heard the news of freedom…you have a severe case of non-wired faith with serious internal conflict.

Following the same idea, when the five integral dimensions of faith are in sync—fully aligned in one belief and operating without conflict—you are genuinely operating in faith. In Mark 11:22-24, Jesus pointed that when you decree something without doubting (doubt is a feeling produced by your thoughts and images) it will be done to you. He also revealed that the secret to successful prayer is to believe you *already* received the object of your desire; when you do, you will surely have it.

Indeed, I am exploring the concept of *hardwired faith* to help you process and apply the message of this book—the Lovesick God—but *hardwired faith* can be used (and is used daily) for anything and everything.

Let's examine each dimension in more detail.

The Creative Power of Your Thoughts

For as he thinks within himself, so he is… (Proverbs 23:7 NASU).

Be careful what you think, because your thoughts run your life (Proverbs 4:23 NCV).

Thinking is the first dimension of faith. Your belief process starts with just one line—a single thought followed by a similar one. Your thoughts are creative; they are an incredible source of spiritual energy. Although invisible, they are a force, a vibrating substance similar to electricity. Scientists affirm that thought moves at the speed of light—it travels at the rate of 186,000 miles per second—that's 930,000 times faster than the sound of your voice. No other force in nature is that fast.

Your mind is like fertile soil that continually grows the seeds you sow. Those seeds are your thoughts. Positive or negative, good or bad, you will harvest them. In brief, whatever you consistently think in your mind must grow; nothing can stop it.

Perhaps you are drowning in a sea of depressing thoughts. You read all the previous chapters but nothing connects—you still feel hopeless. I am here to tell you *there is hope*. You can rewire your brain and reprogram your mind. No, I'm not trying to insert some recycled psychology concepts. I'm referring to the renewing of the mind—a crystal-clear doctrine from the apostle Paul recorded in the New Testament.

> *Do not be conformed to this world, but be transformed by the renewing of your mind, that you may prove what is that good and acceptable and perfect will of God* (Romans 12:2).

> *...but let God transform you into a new person by changing the way you think...* (Romans 12:2 NLT).

Transformation begins with your thoughts. Yes, your mind can be renewed, but you must start deliberately pondering what God thinks of you, how He sees you, and what He feels for you.

Try it now. Meditate on Jesus' affection for you and how the Father desires you. Continue to dwell in God's love for as long as you can, and every time a condemning thought comes, take it captive to the obedience of Christ (see 2 Cor. 10:5).

The Incredible Movie Theater of Your Soul

And the Lord God formed man of the dust of the ground, and breathed into his nostrils the breath of life; and man became a living being (Genesis 2:7).

God breathes and man becomes a living being. We have been made in the image of God—He imagined us and spoke us into existence. Have you considered the infinite ramifications of being an image-bearer?

We are *beings*. What does it mean to be a living being? It means to have the breath of life within us. It means to have creative capabilities. At a lower but significant rate, we can create things, situations, and emotional states. We do this by employing the imagination—the creative visual department of our brains.

Astounding as it sounds, you can give the "breath of life" within you the expression you desire. Not to mention that you do it every day. *Let me explain.*

You are always watching the incredible movie theater of your soul, and you are the producer and main character of your movies. It may be unconsciously, but you play these motion pictures to feel and perceive your immediate future.

Your imagination flows from your thoughts. Actually, your focused thoughts produce the films within. I'll prove it. Read the following paragraph with all your attention:

> I left my red guitar standing on the white snow outside, leaning on the garage wall. Trying to escape the snowstorm, I hurried inside my warm and inviting home. That's when it happened—the captivating aroma of fresh coffee captured my senses and ushered me into a dream-like state. I must confess, I completely forgot about my red guitar. It was not until the night fell, as I went outside to empty my overflowing trash can, that I saw her. She wasn't red anymore. You could almost hear the ice resounding through her strings—

she was trembling in the dark, faithfully standing…but absolutely covered in white.

I'm sure you'll agree that my made-up story is noticeably sensory and visual. What happened within your mind when I told you about my red guitar? You probably pictured a red guitar standing on the white snow, felt my warm, inviting home, and almost savored the aroma of fresh coffee. Did you smell and envision my overflowing trash can? Could you imagine my red guitar trembling in the dark, completely covered in white? Now let me ask you—where did you watch all of that? You saw it within the incredible movie theater of your soul.

Here is how your imagination works with the faith process:

> *Therefore I say to you, all things for which you pray and ask, believe that you have received them, and they will be granted you* (Mark 11:24 NASU).

Notice Jesus using the past verb tense—*received*. How can you believe you have already received what you are praying for? Let me rephrase it—*how can you be certain you already have what you are hoping for?* The easiest way would be to imagine yourself in possession of the thing you are praying for. In simple words, you visualize yourself already living in the circumstances you are expecting to happen.

Two more questions. Can you imagine yourself as the object of God's desire? Can you see yourself as the focus of His love and the treasure of His heart? If you can, you are beginning to believe the life-changing truth about the Lovesick God.

Feelings—Your Harmonic and Magnetic Frequency

Keep thy heart with all diligence; for out of it are the issues of life (Proverbs 4:23 KJV).

Above all else, guard your heart, for it is the well-spring of life (Proverbs 4:23 NIV).

Guard your heart above all else, for it determines the course of your life (Proverbs 4:23 NLT).

Keeping the heart is a matter of life or death, because that's where thoughts and imaginations are born. Your feelings emanate from the current ideas and pictures you're having, and it might come as a surprise, but your surroundings respond to the frequency of your emotions (vibrations).

Don't be scared of the term *vibration*. Just because new agers and metaphysical gurus are using the word doesn't mean it is evil. Just as clapping your hands is not evil, even though is used in devil worship. Scientifically, your feelings *are* vibrations—the oscillating and reciprocating motions of your soul.

The whole universe vibrates. Everything is energy at the core, and everything has a frequency set. The walls, your chair, your pastor, your mother-in-law, the moon, the trees, cats, dogs, and anything you can think of. *Matter* might look solid, but put it under a powerful enough microscope and you'll see how it vibrates according to its frequency set.

In the world of sound, there's a phenomenon called *resonance*. Resonance is the state of a system in which an abnormally large vibration is produced in *response* to an external stimulus. Resonance occurs when the frequency of the stimulus is the same, or nearly the same, as the natural vibration frequency of the original system. *In simple words*—put a cello on the other side of the room and I can make one of its strings resound (vibrate) by playing the right note in the piano. *How can I do this?* By playing the same frequency (at a high volume), I attract the sound from the string and connect both—piano and cello.

Resonance happens all the time, not only in music bands, but in everyday life. It is why I consider our *emotions* as powerful as our *confession*—because they are the signals we are sending out. Once again, like Jesus said, *"It shall be done to you according to your faith"* (Matt. 9:29 NASU). It is "done to you" because you attract and connect to whatever you are in harmony with—whatever you are vibrating toward.

What you continually feel is what you believe. *I will say it again*—what you feel is the proof of your present belief. Your emotions are the interpretation and expression of your faith.

Do you realize how powerful this is? Do you feel you will have a horrible day? *You will.* Do you feel it will be fantastic? *It will be fantastic.* Because according to your faith it is done to you. Of course bad events happen, but you always control the response—you always manage your "resonance."

Do you feel that God is disappointed and mad at you? Then you will live under a cloud of depression. Do you feel that God is lovesick for you and that the Father loves you as much as He loves Jesus? Then, the truth of His love will gradually set you free from all fear, guilt, shame, and reproach.

Words—Your Ability to Create, Decree, and Establish

> …*"The word is near you, in your mouth and in your heart"* (that is, the word of faith which we preach): *that if you confess with your mouth the Lord Jesus and believe in your heart that God has raised Him from the dead, you will be saved. For with the heart one believes unto righteousness, and with the mouth confession is made unto salvation* (Romans 10:8-10).

How did you get saved? According to Paul, you got saved by using a powerful law of the Kingdom—the word of faith. You confessed Jesus and truly believed in your heart that God raised Him from the dead. The believing in your heart is the combination of the first three dimensions of faith—*thoughts, mental images, and feelings.* When those three areas are combined with confession, salvation happens.

Do you think the law of the word of faith ends there? Not at all! As with the previous dimensions, the word of faith works all the time and for everything. The word of faith is creative. It brings into existence what we believe and expect—good or bad. You can curse yourself or bless yourself. You can curse your kids or bless them. You can build others or destroy them.

But here's the catch—your words possess this amazing power *only* when they are backed by your thoughts, images, and feelings. Confession without the first three dimensions is like a car without gasoline or like an eagle without wings.

You should pay close attention to *your* words—especially to those backed by vivid imagination and strong emotions—because *your* words will return to you; they will accomplish *your* purpose, complete the assignment you gave them, and never comeback empty-handed. Yes, at a lower degree but similar to your Maker. You were made in His image, remember?

Just as rain and snow descend from the skies and don't go back until they've watered the earth, doing their work of making things grow and blossom, producing seed for farmers and food for the hungry, so will the words that come out of My mouth not come back empty-handed. They'll do the work I sent them to do, they'll complete the assignment I gave them (Isaiah 55:10-11 MSG).

One more thing—your confession also serves as stabilizer. If your thoughts, images, and feelings are out of control, you can conquer your mind with your words. Speak the word of faith; confess yourself into another reality. You can do like King David, who questioned and challenged his negative emotions with praise. Yes, David practiced self-talk:

> *Why are you cast down, O my soul? And why are you disquieted within me? Hope in God; for I shall yet praise Him, the help of my countenance and my God* (Psalms 42:11).

Actions—the Confirmation and Proof of Your Faith

> *Faith by itself, if it does not have works, is dead. But someone will say, "You have faith, and I have works." Show me your faith without your works,*

and I will show you my faith by my works....Was not Abraham our father justified by works when he offered Isaac his son on the altar? Do you see that faith was working together with his works, and by works faith was made perfect? (James 2:17-18;21-22)

Your works are the evidence of what you believe—actions confirm the ways of your heart. We can fake our reality with empty words, but our works will tell the truth. Actions don't lie (most of the time). That's why Jesus assured us that we could identify the tree by the fruit.

The apostle James reveals that faith is proven and made perfect by works. Abraham proved his faith with obedience when he determined to obey the Lord and sacrifice Isaac. Actually, he became so committed to obey that God had to stop him before the knife reached his son.

In one of the most heartrending stories of the Gospels, we find a woman proving her faith by her actions:

A woman in the crowd had suffered for twelve years with constant bleeding. She had suffered a great deal from many doctors.... She had heard about Jesus, so she came up behind Him through the crowd and touched His robe. For she thought to herself, "If I can just touch His robe, I will be healed." Immediately the bleeding stopped, and she could feel in her body that she had been healed of her terrible condition (Mark 5:25-29 NLT).

The story illustrates four dimensions of hardwired faith—*thoughts, images, feelings, and actions*. Before breaking through the crowd and touching Jesus' garment, "*she thought to herself*"; other translations simply state "*she said.*" Put differently, she imagined and felt her healing before reaching out. Then, she confirmed the vision with her works, pushing her way through a hectic Middle Eastern crowd.

Have in mind that under Jewish law, she was unclean and forbidden to touch people. To prove her faith with actions, this woman overcame numerous emotional barriers and regulations. But it was worth it. It worked; her faith healed her.

You might say, "Pablo, the Lord Jesus healed her." Technically, yes. But that's not what Jesus said:

He said to her, "Daughter, your faith has healed you. Go in peace and be freed from your suffering" (Mark 5:34 NIV).

Clearly, Jesus wanted to highlight her remarkable faith. He could have stated, "My power has healed you," but instead He declared, *"...your faith has healed you."*

What does all this mean to you? It means that your faith can heal you—externally and internally.

Consider once again the ravished heart of God and how He desires you. Imagine Jesus telling you, "I have loved you as My Father has loved Me" (see John 15:9). Let the flame of His love so capture your mind and emotions that you begin to *act* and *live* as the beloved of God. Continue drinking from the river of His affections, certain to be the delight of His heart, and observe what happens. See if your soul remains broken and lost. You might soon discover that your faith has healed you.

In summary, simply knowing how much God desires you will bring some relief, but truly believing His affections for you will change you forever. I encourage you to read this chapter on hardwired faith often. It will help you greatly.

Next: Becoming Lovesick for God

As we approach the end of the age, the Lord is raising up a generation of lovesick worshipers. They will live fascinated with the beauty of Jesus and grow every day more lovesick for Him.

I have asked myself, how can the Person of Jesus become my magnificent obsession? How can I develop a lovesick heart and desire Him as He desires me? How can the beauty of His majesty take such a hold of my imagination that I would not desire other lovers nor seek to worship the gods of this age?

I am still searching for a comprehensive answer, but would you like to learn what I found so far?

CHAPTER TEN

Becoming Lovesick for God

For we did not follow cunningly devised fables when we made known to you the power and coming of our Lord Jesus Christ, but were eyewitnesses of His majesty....And we heard this voice which came from heaven when we were with Him on the holy mountain (2 Peter 1:16,18).

It happened on a high and glorious mountain—Jesus' face shone like the sun and His clothes became as white as light. Things kept escalating as Moses and Elijah joined the reunion to talk with Him. All of this made Peter very excited; it appeared to be *the* conversation he was born to join. I mean, Jesus talking with the *law* and the *prophets*—this was surely destiny. Unfortunately, we don't know what Jesus, Moses, and Elijah were discussing, but we have record of Peter's brilliant idea: *"Master, this is a great moment! What would you think if I built three memorials here on the mountain—one for you, one for Moses, one for Elijah?"* (Matt. 17:4 MSG). Why not capitalize this heavenly moment with three sacred tabernacle shrines? Believe it or not, his ingenious proposal got interrupted by the Father:

> *While he was going on like this, babbling, a light-radiant cloud enveloped them, and sounding from deep in the cloud a voice: "This is My Son, marked by My love, focus of My delight. Listen to Him"* (Matthew 17:5 MSG).

Instantly the three disciples fell to the ground, absolutely terrified. Perhaps John whispered to Peter, "I told you to shut up; you always have to say something." (OK, I admit I'm often picking on Peter—I'm sure the day we meet in Heaven he'll remind me of every silly thing I ever said!)

Becoming Eyewitnesses
of His Majesty

Here is the point. Several years after that glorious event on Transfiguration Mountain, Peter recalled the experience with one of the most stunning sentences of Scripture: "[We] *were eyewitnesses of His majesty*" (2 Pet. 1:16). I can't find a better phrase that describes the quest ahead of us.

If our aim is to be lovesick for God, being eyewitnesses of His majesty must become our obsession—fellowshipping with Him, listening to His voice, beholding His beauty, and consistently dwelling in the holy mountain (God's presence).

King David comes to mind. If there is a man who became lovesick for God, it was he. Consider his famous song, *"One thing I have desired of the Lord, that will I seek…"* (Ps. 27:4). Those words reveal the dream of his heart—to behold the beauty of the Lord, to be an eyewitness of His majesty.

David's motive for dwelling *was* beholding. His dream was not the house of the Lord but experiencing the Lord of the house. He wanted to *be* there all the days of his life, because the tabernacle (God's manifest presence) was there and he loved to gaze upon the beauty of the Lord and drink from the river of His pleasures (see Ps. 36:7-9).

How about you? Would you like to develop a "beholding His beauty" and "eyewitness of His majesty" lifestyle?

How to Develop and Cultivate a Lovesick Heart

I could explore essential spiritual disciplines like prayer, fasting, devotional study, communion, walking in holiness, practicing "fast repentance," developing a lifestyle of worship, etc. I've chosen, however, to focus on the truths that will motivate and fuel your heart to practice those spiritual disciplines.

Here is why: Knowing what to do is *not* enough. As stated in the first chapter, your heart craves for pleasure and experience. Faced with the pressure of emptiness, you will consistently pursue that which you believe can bring you happiness, adventure, romance, meaning, and fulfillment.

The greatest pleasure you can experience *is* spiritual, pure, and eternal. It's the ever-growing pleasure of encountering Jesus as the Bridegroom God—feeling His burning heart intoxicating your soul with the flame of love.

Having that in mind, how can I increase the quantity and intensity of my encounters? To do that, we must understand a life-changing law that Paul revealed to the Corinthians. Practicing this law will save you years of frustration and rapidly develop passion for Jesus within your heart.

Through the years I received glimpses of this *law* from different teachers. In my opinion, no one makes it clearer than Mike Bickle—he explains the law as "the beholding and becoming principle." Basically, the beholding and becoming principle states that whatever we behold or understand about God's heart toward us is what we become in our hearts toward God.

> *But we all, with unveiled face, beholding as in a mirror the glory of the Lord, are being transformed into the same image from glory to glory, just as by the Spirit of the Lord* (2 Corinthians 3:18).

If you want to become lovesick for God, begin to put the ancient law to work—you will grow lovesick by beholding the glory of the One who is lovesick for you. The more you feel the flame of God's love, the more you will love Him in return; the more you behold the beauty of Jesus and come to understand *why* He's beautiful, the more lovesick you will become.

> *We love Him because He first loved us* (1 John 4:19).

Here is the same powerful principle with different phrasing. Like Paul, John reveals the key to spiritual transformation: *We love God because He first loved us.* This means the only way to truly love God is to first receive and understand His love for us. When we see it in Him, the same reality is awakened within.

Do you want more passion for Jesus? You have to first experience His passion for you. Do you want more dedication for God? Encounter Jesus at the Cross and discover how dedicated He is toward you. Do you want to enjoy God? Discover how much He enjoys you. The list goes on; whatever virtue you desire in your spiritual life must be first encountered in God's heart. That's how it works. Actually, that's the only way it works.

It's impossible to live the Christian life without a heart awakened by love. Rules and regulations work wonders—they provide wisdom and keep you on the way—but they can never ignite your soul with burning desire. Human zeal, willpower, inspired ideas, enthusiasm—they're all beneficial—but they are not able to sustain your soul long term. Only your Maker can. And only His Spirit can transform you from glory to glory into the same image (character, person) you are beholding.

To sum up, let's turn to the Song of Solomon. The Bride declares she is *lovesick* for her Beloved on two occasions—first she is lovesick by understanding and feeling the fire of His love; second, she becomes lovesick by experiencing His transcendent beauty.

I intend to close this book by highlighting the fire of God's love. As for the transcendent beauty of Jesus... well, the subject is so amazing that it deserves a future book.

Exceptionally Better Than the Wine of This World

Oh, that he would kiss me with the kisses of His mouth! For your love is more delightful than wine. The fragrance of your perfume is intoxicating; your name is perfume poured out... (Song of Solomon 1:2-3 HCSB).

The most excellent song ever written begins with the Bride's cry for intimacy. She asks for the kisses of His mouth (God's Word) to touch the deepest places of her heart. Obviously, she has experienced before how those kisses unveil God's emotions. That's why her next statement is: *"For Your love is more delightful than wine."* Encountering God's affections for her tasted way better than the fallen wine of this world.

Wine "exhilarates" the heart; it's a stimulating drink that makes people happy. It symbolizes the intoxicating things of this world—good and bad. There is the *good wine* of God's blessings and also the *bad wine* of our sin. We all know sin is pleasurable. In fact, it appears to be the most pleasurable thing our souls can taste until we experience the superior pleasures of the Gospel—the delight of being loved by God and of feeling His living flame burning inside.

Nonetheless, by stating, "Your love is better than wine," the Bride is implying more than, "Your love is better than sin." She means that experiencing God's love is better than all the other privileges of life and better than any other experience in the natural realm.

He brought me to the banquet hall, and He looked on me with love. Sustain me with raisins; refresh

me with apricots, for I am lovesick (Song of Solomon 2:4-5 HCSB).

At the wedding table (banqueting hall), the Bride
gets drunk with the Bridegroom's love. She asks to be
sustained and refreshed—she is lovesick, she can't live
without Him, and she is never going back to *usual*. She's
ruined by God's affections.

Have you ever been in love? Lovesickness is like falling in love; you can't go back to "business as usual," and
you can't be unresponsive or pretend nothing happened.
When you're lovesick, your affections are stolen, your
thought life and imagination are captured, your longings
and preferences change—the way you use your time, your
money, your expectations for the future. Actually, every
fiber of your being is influenced by the deep emotions you
feel for the one you love.

Loving God With All Your Heart, Soul, and Mind

*Jesus said to him, "You shall love the Lord your
God with all your heart, with all your soul, and*

with all your mind." This is the first and great commandment (Matthew 22:37-38).

This first and great commandment is not only a commandment, but a prophecy. Before the end of the age, the Bride of Christ will love the Lord with every fiber of her being. King Jesus is returning for a lovesick Bride who agrees with His ways, burns with holy desire, and is ready to rule and reign with Him.

Restoring the first commandment to first place is the Lord's agenda behind every move of His Spirit—that we would love the Lord with all our hearts, all our souls, all our minds, and all our strength (see Deut. 6:5; Matt. 22:37-38). When you become lovesick for God, the first commandment is restored to first place in your life.

The Journey Ahead

You were created to experience the everlasting encounter with the Lovesick God—made to live fascinated and ravished by the flame of His love. *This is who you are.* I have only reminded you of things that are written within and of all the treasures available for your heart.

Today, you can cross the threshold into a vibrant love relationship with the Son of God. Why settle for mediocrity when you can experience His fullness? You are meant to live a wholehearted life in full union with God.

Take a deep breath now, open the eyes of your heart and behold your Maker—He is eternally lovesick for you.

About Pablo Pérez

Pablo Pérez and his wife Andrea are based in Kansas City, Missouri, where he serves as one of the leaders at the International House of Prayer. He is also director of Encounter God Ministries and the founder of Encounter-GodUniversity.com, an online training facility for those who desire to love Jesus as the Father loves Him (see John. 17:26).

IN THE RIGHT HANDS, THIS BOOK WILL CHANGE LIVES!

Most of the people who need this message will not be looking for this book. To change their lives, you need to put a copy of this book in their hands.

> *But others (seeds) fell into good ground, and brought forth fruit, some a hundred-fold, some sixty-fold, some thirty-fold* (Matthew 13:8).

Our ministry is constantly seeking methods to find the good ground, the people who need this anointed message to change their lives. Will you help us reach these people?

> *Remember this—a farmer who plants only a few seeds will get a small crop. But the one who plants generously will get a generous crop* (2 Corinthians 9:6).

EXTEND THIS MINISTRY BY SOWING 3 BOOKS, 5 BOOKS, 10 BOOKS, OR MORE TODAY, AND BECOME A LIFE CHANGER!

Thank you,

Don Nori Sr., Founder
Destiny Image
Since 1982

DESTINY IMAGE PUBLISHERS, INC.

"Promoting Inspired Lives."

VISIT OUR NEW SITE HOME AT
WWW.DESTINYIMAGE.COM

FREE SUBSCRIPTION TO DI NEWSLETTER

Receive free unpublished articles by top DI authors, exclusive discounts, and free downloads from our best and newest books.

Visit www.destinyimage.com to subscribe.

Write to: Destiny Image
             P.O. Box 310
             Shippensburg, PA 17257-0310

Call: 1-800-722-6774

Email: orders@destinyimage.com

For a complete list of our titles or to place an order
online, visit www.destinyimage.com.

FIND US ON FACEBOOK OR FOLLOW US ON TWITTER.

www.facebook.com/destinyimage   facebook
www.twitter.com/destinyimage   twitter